# DUINO ELEGIES

# DUINO

# ELEGIES

## Rainer Maria Rilke
## Translated by Gary Miranda

Breitenbush Books          Portland, Oregon

Library of Congress Number 01-67299
ISBN (paper) 0-932576-08-7
ISBN (deluxe cloth) 0-932576-07-9

Breitenbush Books are published for James Anderson
by Breitenbush Publications.
Mailing address P.O. Box 02137. Portland, Oregon 97202.
Printed in the USA by Press-22, Portland, Oregon.

For Charlene O'Connor

*If I don't manage to fly, someone else will.*
*The Spirit wants only that there be flying.*
*As for who happens to do it,*
*in that he has only a passing interest.*

Rainer Maria Rilke

(from a letter, dated 27 December 1913, to Princess Marie von Thurn und Taxis-Hohenlohe, to whom the *Duino Elegies*, begun one year earlier and completed nine years later, are dedicated).

# DUINO ELEGIES

# First Elegy

What angel, if I called out, would hear me?
And even if one of them impulsively embraced me,
I'd be crushed by its strength. For beauty
is just the beginning of a terror we can barely stand:
we admire it because it calmly refuses to crush us.
Every angel terrifies. And so I control myself,
choking back the dark impulse to cry.

But who, then, can help us? Not angels, not men.
And the animals, instinctively, have already noticed
that we aren't really at home in our talked-about world.
So we're left with, say, some tree on a hillside—

one that we see every day; we're left with yesterday's
stroll and the pampered loyalty of an old habit
that liked us so much it decided to stay, and never left.

And the night—the night, when the worldmouth of the wind
gnaws at our faces. But who wouldn't she stay for,
that sought-after, softly deceiving night
who wearily awaits the lonely stranger?
You think the nighttime is easier on lovers?
All they do is use each other to hide their fates
from themselves. When are you going to learn?
Take the emptiness you hold in your arms
and scatter it into the open spaces we breathe:
maybe the birds will feel how the air is thinner,
and fly with more affection.

All right, the springtime did need you. And lots of stars
wanted you to watch them. A wave, long-gone now,
seemed to lift itself just for you, as did the strains
from some violin when you passed an open window.
All this was entrusted to you. But how did you handle it?
Isn't it true that you were always distracted,
expecting something else, as though these things
were announcing some lover's arrival?
(Where did you think you were going to keep her,
what with all those strange thoughts coming and going
inside you—not to mention spending the night!)

Instead, when you're lonely, praise the great lovers:
the fame of their loving still isn't known enough.
The abandoned ones—how you almost envied them,
they seemed so far above those others, whose love
was answered. You can't praise them enough, but try.
Start over. Remember: a hero is immortal
because even his downfall was a play for survival,
a final birth. But the great lovers exhaust nature:
she has to take them back into herself, as though
she weren't strong enough to create them a second time.
Have you praised Gaspara Stampa enough—
so that any girl deserted by a lover would feel,
in the face of such an example: If only I
could be like her! Shouldn't these oldest hurts,
by now, be bearing more fruit in us? Isn't it time
that our loving freed us from the one we love
so that we, however shaken, endured—just as the arrow,
drawn, endures the bowstring, anxious to become
*more* than itself? Because staying is nowhere.

Voices, voices. Heart, listen—as before this
only saints have listened: the power of that voice
lifted them right off the ground and still,
impossible as ever, they kept on kneeling,
not even noticing—they were listening so hard.
I don't mean that you could survive the voice of God—
not at all. But notice the breathing,

the continuous message that emerges from silence.
Even now it rasps toward you from the mouths
of all those who died young. In Rome, in Naples,
whenever you entered a church, you would feel
their fate, that quiet message. Or else
some inscription overhead would remind you of it—
like the plaque you recently saw in Santa Maria Formosa.
What do they want of me? That I kindly remove my look
of suffered injustice, which sometimes tends
to prevent their spirits from speaking clearly:

True, it's strange not to live on the earth any more,
not to continue customs you were just getting used to,
not to interpret roses and other such promising things
as omens of future happiness, not to be what you were,
cared for by infinitely anxious hands, and to put
even your name aside, like some broken toy.
Strange, not to wish wishes any more. Strange
to see what once seemed so securely fastened together
fluttering randomly in space. And it's exhausting
being dead—so many things to catch up on
before you experience a little eternity. Still,
the living are all mistaken when they make the distinctions
too sharp. Angels, it's said, sometimes don't even know
if they're moving among the living or the dead.
In both realms the flood of eternity rushes forever
over all the ages and, in both, drowns out the voices.

The ones taken from us early no longer need us, finally.
You gradually get used to being away from the things
of earth, just as you gradually turned from the breasts
of your mother. But we, who need such powerful secrets,
we who tend to advance in joy only through sorrow,
could we survive without them? And what about the legend
of the mourning for Linos: how it was music
that first dared to break that rigid silence,
how only then—in the startled space from which death
had snatched the godlike youth forever—
could the emptiness begin to vibrate with that sound
which even now delights us, comforts us, helps?

## Second Elegy

Every angel terrifies. Still, though I know
how almost-deadly you are, you birds of the soul,
I call out to you. Whatever happened to the days
of Tobias, when one of the most radiant of you
stood in the simple doorway, only slightly disguised
for the trip, and didn't seem frightening at all?
The young man peeked out, curious,
and mistook you for just another young man.
But if that same angel today, threatening,
should take even a step from behind the stars
and move in our direction, the hammering
of our own hearts would kill us. Who are you?

Fortunate firstborns, favorites of creation,
mountain ranges whose peaks were reddened
by the first morning, pollen of a blossoming God,
hinges of light, corridors stairways thrones
and spaces constructed of sheer existence,
shields of delight, roaring storms of rapture
and, suddenly, singly, *mirrors*, drawing back
into their faces the very beauty they've spilt.

We—we evaporate in our feelings. We exhale ourselves
and vanish. Our scent grows fainter as it passes
from ember to ember. Someone may say to us:
"Yes. You've gotten into my blood. This room,
the springtime—it's full of you." But what for?
It can't hold us. We vanish in and around it.
And even those who are beautiful—can anyone keep them
from vanishing? The appearance of beauty
seems fixed in their faces for always, and, always,
it fades. Everything we are evaporates—
like dew from the spring grass, or steam from hot food.
A smile—where does it go! A glance—new, warm,
a gesture of the heart—oh it hurts to say it,
but this is what we *are*! Does the universe taste
of us then, since we spill ourselves into it?
Do the angels really retrieve only what is theirs,
what has spilt from them, or do they at times,
by accident, get a little of our existence mixed in?

—Just a little, mixed in with their features,
like that certain look on the faces of pregnant women
which they don't even notice as they spiral back
into themselves. (And why *should* they notice?)

Lovers, if they knew it, could say marvelous things
in the night air. But it seems that everything
wants to keep us a secret. Look: the trees, they exist;
the houses we live in still stand. And yet
we pass it all by like an exchange of breath.
And it all agrees to ignore us—half out of shame,
perhaps, and half from some secret hope.

You lovers, so self-satisfied, I ask you about us.
You hold each other. But where's your proof?
Look, sometimes my hands happen to find and hold
each other, or my worn-out face finds refuge
in being held by them. This gives me a slight sensation.
And yet who, just for that, would be brave enough to *exist*?
So I ask you—you who build and build on each other's
excitement until, overwhelmed, one of you cries "No more!";
who under each other's hands grow fuller and fuller,
like vintage years; who sometimes sink back,
but only because the other completely takes over—
I ask you about us. I know why touching each other
gives you such pleasure: because caressing staves off
something; because the place you cover so tenderly

doesn't vanish; because you sense the pure permanence
beneath it. And so every embrace seems to promise
eternity. But really, once you've survived that first
shock of encounter, and the gazing from windows,
and the first walk together in the garden,
that can happen just once—lovers, are you really
these things any longer? When you raise yourselves
to each other's lips—a drink raised to a drink—
how strangely the role of the drinker seems to get lost!

But think of those Attic steles, how they amazed you.
How cautious those human gestures seemed. How gently
love and parting rested on the shoulders, as though
they were made of other stuff than what we know.
Remember the hands, how they touched without pressure,
despite the strength you could see in the torsos.
Self-controlled, they knew: we have come this far;
this much is ours, to touch each other just so.
The gods may press down harder on us.
But that's the concern of the gods.

If only *we* could attain such pure, restrained humanity.
If only we could find our own little strip of fertile land,
with a river on one side and rocks on the other.
For *our* heart too is always escaping. And we can't
look after it in soothing pictures any more,
or in godlike bodies, that teach it greater control.

# Third Elegy

It's one thing to write love poems. Another, though,
to deal with that river-god of the blood: hidden, guilty.
Even the girl, who thinks she knows her young lover,
even she isn't close enough for him to tell
how this lord of lust—in the lonely times
before she knew him, before she eased him, almost
before she seemed possible—would lift up his godhead,
wet with the unknowable, and churn the night
to an endless riot. Such a Neptune in the blood,
with his three-pronged weapon! Such a dark wind
in the chest out of that twisted conch! Listen:
the night is becoming a cave, emptying itself.

Stars, perhaps it's from you that the lover's desire
for the face of his loved one grows; perhaps he
responds to her pure look because he remembers yours.
But it wasn't you, and it wasn't his mother,
who arched his brows into that look of readiness.
It wasn't your mouth, girl—though you hold him—
it wasn't yours that made his own mouth curve
with new ripeness. Do you really think
that your gentle arrival could shatter him so—
you, who move with the softness of a morning breeze?
True, you surprised his heart. But older fears
swept in when your touch startled him. Call him:
you can't distract him completely from those dark
associations. He tries, and he does escape them,
and, relieved, he makes your deepest self his home,
enters, and decides to begin himself new there.
But when did he ever begin himself really?

Mother, *you* made him once, tiny; you began him;
he was new with you. You shaped a friendly world
for his new eyes, shutting the strange one out.
But where did they go—those years when your slight frame
was enough to eclipse a whole world of chaos?
You protected him from so much: at night
you made the threatening bedroom safe; your caring
filled up the space of his night, and made it human.
You placed the nightlight not in the darkness,

but in your closer presence, and it shone like a friend.
There wasn't a creak you couldn't explain away
with a smile—almost as though you expected the floor
to behave that way. And he listened, and it soothed him.
You accomplished so much, so gently, just by rising
and coming to him. His tall, shrouded fate
retreated behind the dresser; his unruly future,
disgruntled, adjusted itself to the folds of the curtain.

And he himself, as he lay there comforted,
drowsily mixing the sweet taste of your presence
with the first taste of sleep, *seemed*
to be well-protected. But *inside*—who, there,
could hold back or channel the flood of his origin?
For he had no sense of fear, asleep.
Sleeping, dreaming, in a kind of fever,
how he wandered off. He—innocent, shy—
how tangled he became in the clinging weeds
of his inner self, already thick with twisted designs,
with clutching undergrowth, with the shapes
of prowling animals. How he surrendered to,
how he loved it! Loved his inner world,
his wilderness within, that primitive jungle inside
where his heart, shimmering green, stood
amid speechless debris. Loved! Passed through it
and, following his roots, arrived at the violent
source where his own birth was already irrelevant.

Descended with love into the older blood,
the ravines where monsters waited, still gorged
with his forefathers. And every monster recognized
him, winked at him, knew. Yes, Horror itself
smiled at him. You've seldom smiled so tenderly, Mother.
And how could he not love it, if it smiled at him!
Before he loved *you* he loved it: even while
you carried him in your womb it was there,
dissolved in the water that cushions the seed.

Look, we don't love, like the flowers, from a single
season. When we love, a sap that has flowed
for countless ages stirs up in our arms. Yes,
girl—*this*: that we've loved *within* ourselves,
not one, not someone we're about to meet,
but the numberless comings-into-being;
not one child only, but all the fathers
who live in our depths like crumbled mountains,
but the parched riverbeds of previous mothers,
but the whole soundless landscape of destiny,
cloudy or cloudless—*this*, girl, was here before you.

And you yourself—how could you know
what an ancient past you awoke in your lover?
What emotions flared up from beings no longer here!
What women inside him hated you! What sinister
men you aroused in his young veins! Dead children

stretched out their hands to you. . .Oh
gently, gently, show him the steady love
in a daily task, attract him toward the garden,
make him a gift of the irresistible nights. . . .

Hold him. . .back.

## Fourth Elegy

The trees of our lives—when will their winter come?
We can't agree on it. Unlike migratory birds,
we don't know it by instinct. Out of season and late,
we suddenly throw ourselves into the wind,
landing in some indifferent pond. We're no sooner
conscious of blooming than we're conscious of withering.
And to think that lions still roam somewhere,
so used to being magnificent
that they don't even know what weakness is.

But we, even completely intent on one thing,
always feel the pinch of another. Resentment

is our middle name. Don't lovers always overstep
the boundaries of each other's lives, promising
room to breathe, adventure, a place of their own?
Then, painfully, a thumbnail sketch of the background
is added for contrast, and we see them;
they're very clear to us. We don't know the shape
of our own feeling, but only what shapes it
from the outside.

Which of us hasn't sat anxiously before the curtain
of his own heart? Up it goes. The stage is set
for a scene of parting. Easy enough to understand.
The inevitable garden, the props swaying a little
as the dancer starts to enter. . . .
But wait—*he's* not the one! No matter how easily
he pretends, he's nothing more than a civil servant
in disguise, the kind who enters his house by the kitchen.
I've got no use for these actors who only half fill
their masks. I'd rather have a puppet—at least
it's whole. I'll put up with the hollow body
and the strings and the face that's all surface.
Look—I'm out here waiting, and even if
the footlights go out and a voice says "That's all!"—
even if nothing comes my way from the stage
but the grey breeze of emptiness—even if none
of my silent ancestors will sit by me any more—
not a woman, not even the kid with the brown squinty eye—

even then I'll stay. I can always stare.

Aren't I right, Father? You who found the taste
of life so bitter because you sampled mine,
that first confusing taste of what I would have to do,
who kept on sampling it as I grew older and,
fascinated by the after-taste of my strange future,
kept trying to fathom that vague stare of mine—
yes, you, my father, who so often since your death
have been inside me, worrying about the things
I hoped for, trading that peace that the dead have earned,
whole kingdoms of peace, for my tiny piece of fate—
aren't I right? And both of you, who used to love me
for the small beginnings of love I showed you
and which I always lost track of because it seemed
that the distance in your faces, even while I loved them,
became so wide you weren't there any more—
aren't I right when I feel like this
waiting in front of the puppet show, staring so hard
at it, in fact, that in order to balance my stare
an angel finally has to come as one of the actors
and bring the puppet's body to life?

Angel and puppet. So now we *are* going to have a play.
So now, here, we can put together what we're always
taking apart. So now, for the first time,
the cycle that works in the whole order of things

can apply to *our* seasons as well. So now,
over and above us, the angel is playing.
Look, the dying—surely *they* can figure out
how full of deception this all is, what we're doing here—
here where nothing is what it really is.
Oh for those times as a child, when there was more
behind each shape than just the past, and the future
didn't exist. True, we were growing up, and sometimes
we even tried to grow up faster, half out of love
for those who had nothing left but being grown up.
Still, when we went off by ourselves, we were content
with the never-changing, and we stood there
in a place between world and toy, on a spot that had,
from the very beginning, been destined for a pure event.

But who'll describe a child just as he is?
Who'll put him in a constellation and let him
measure the distances with his hand?
Who'll make the death of a child out of bread
that's grey and getting hard—or leave it
inside his round mouth like the core of a lovely apple. . . ?
A murderer's mind is easy to understand. But this:
death, your whole death—and even *before* you've lived—
to hold it inside you so gently and without resentment—
this is beyond description!

## Fifth Elegy

But what are *they* doing here, these acrobats,
a little more fugitive, even, than us?
Who are they trying to please? What sadistic will
compels them from earliest childhood to perform
such violent contortions? It wrings them,
bends them, slings them and swings them,
throws them up and catches them: as though the air
were freshly waxed, they slide back down
to this threadbare carpet worn thin by their endless
leaping. And the carpet itself seems lost in space,
stuck on there like a bandage, as though the earth
had scraped itself on the suburban sky.

And no sooner
are they there, standing there on display—
standing *for* display, like a capital "D"—
than the gripping urge returns as always and spins
even the strongest of them away—just for fun—
as August the Strong used to do with a tin platter
at dinner time.

Oh and around this center the audience
blooms and fades, like the petals of a rose.
Around this pestle, this pistil, impregnated
by its own pollen, fertilized once more
for the fake fruit of a boredom no one acknowledges,
a thinly disguised boredom glazed over
with synthetic smiles.

There, the shriveled, withered weight-lifter,
old now, but still good for drumming up business,
shrunken up inside his bulk of skin as though
it contained *two* men—one who now lies in the churchyard,
and this one, who outlived the other, deaf
and sometimes a bit strange in his widowed skin.

And then there's the young man, the leader,
who seems the offspring of a neck and a nun,
tightly packed with muscles and innocence.

Oh but you other two,
looking as though you'd been presented as toys
to a small pain during one of its long convalescences:
you, the boy, who with a thud peculiar to unripened fruit
fall a hundred times a day from the acrobat tree
(which, quicker than water, has spring, summer and fall
in a matter of minutes), landing with a bounce on the grave.
Sometimes you glance at your seldomly tender mother
and a loving look begins on your face—
hesitant, shy, hardly attempted before it spreads itself
over all your body, whose surface quickly absorbs it.
For again the clapping hands of the leader are saying
"Jump down!"—and before that other pain has time
to reach your racing heart and define itself,
the burning in the soles of your feet begins,
forcing up into your eyes a few physical tears.
And yet, blind to it all, the smile. . . .

O Angel, take it! Pick that small-flowered herb of healing!
Preserve it in a vase! Put it with those joys
you're saving for us. Praise it on the delicate vase
with a flowery, soaring inscription:
                              *"Subrisio Saltat."**

*"The Smile of an Acrobat"

And then you, little girl, the sweet one,
you whom even the most tempting joys leap over in silence.
Maybe the fringes of your dress are happy *for* you—
or the green metallic silk over your firm young breasts,
maybe it feels endlessly pampered, in need of nothing.
You,
publicly displayed on shoulders,
always balancing yourself on the swaying scales,
like freshly-stacked fruit in a market.

Oh where is the place I keep in my heart
where they didn't know *how* to balance yet,
where they fell from each other like mating animals
that are badly paired, where the weights are still heavy,
where the sticks continue their stupid spinning
as the platters go wobbling off. . . ?

And suddenly in this tiresome nowhere, suddenly
the indefinable point where obvious Too-little
turns around, changes itself into that empty Too-much.
Where, despite all the digits, the score
adds up to zero.

Places, oh the place in Paris, endless showplace,
where the milliner, Madame LaMort, curls and twists
the restless ways of the world like endless ribbons,
creating the latest in bows, frills, flowers, rosettes

and artificial fruits—all falsely dyed—
to decorate the cheap winter hats of fate.

Angel: suppose there's another place,
one we know nothing about, and suppose that there,
on some wonderful carpet, lovers managed to accomplish
what they're always failing at here—the daring maneuvers
of their high-flying hearts, the pyramids of their pleasure,
ladders leaning only against each other
with no ground underneath, and trembling—
suppose they *could* manage it there, surrounded
by a ring of spectators, the countless silent dead:
wouldn't the dead, then, finally, throw down
the forever-valid coins of happiness they're always
hoarding, always hiding from us—throw them down
in front of that couple whose smile at last
would be real, out there, on that hushed carpet?

## Sixth Elegy

Fig tree: how long you've had meaning for me—
the way you almost skip over the blossoming
and then, without fanfare, pour your pure secret
into the fruit when its time arrives:
your branches bend like the pipes of a fountain,
forcing the sap downwards then up till it leaps
from sleep, only half-awake, to the joy
of its sweetest achievement. Look:
like the god into the swan.
                                        But we
prolong the blossoming, and take such pride in it.
By the time we arrive at the core of our final fruit,

we're already betrayed. Only a few
have that strong impulse to action that allows them
to stand, already perfected and full,
when the urge to blossom comes like a tempting night-breeze,
softly touching the youth of their mouths and their eyelids:
heroes perhaps, and those who die young, those in whom
the gardener, Death, has twisted the veins
in a different direction. These plunge on ahead,
drawing their own smiles behind them,
like that team of chargers in front of the conquering king
in the delicate bas-reliefs at Karnak.

The hero strangely resembles those who die young.
The length of his life doesn't matter to him;
the climb is his whole existence. Again and again
his constant sense of risk takes the shape
of a new constellation, and he enters it.
Few could follow him there. But fate,
which keeps us wrapped in a dark, secret cloud,
grows inspired and sings him into the storm
of its roaring world. I've yet to hear anyone like him
when, in a sudden rushing of air, his ominous tone
goes through me.

And then how gladly I'd hide from this longing.
Oh if only I were a boy, and everything seemed possible—
if only I were propped up in the arms of my future,

reading about Samson, of how his mother at first
bore nothing, and, afterwards, everything.

O Mother, wasn't he a hero already, even inside you?
Didn't it start there, within, that great decision of his?
Thousands converged in the womb, anxious to be him,
but see how he picked and discarded, chose
and was able to do it. And if he tumbled columns,
it was when he broke from the world of your womb
into this narrower world, where he chose
and could do it again.

Oh the mothers of heroes! Sources of raging rivers!
Ravines into which, from the high cliff of the heart,
weeping, you've already cast your girlhood,
to exist from now on for the sons!
For whenever the hero was interrupted by love,
he would storm free, propelled forward
by every heartbeat that claimed him—
until, already turning to go, he'd stand
at the end of the smiles, a stranger.

# Seventh Elegy

Voice, forget the courting, the mating call.
You've outgrown that. Even if you could make it sound
as clear as the bird when the springtime lifts him up
almost forgetting that he's a small nervous thing
and not just a particular heart she's tossing
toward brightness, into the intimate sky.
Just like that, like him, that's how you'd like to call—
so that some mate, even before she saw you,
would feel you and grow hushed, letting her answer
wake slowly and warm itself by listening
until it was the glowing reflection of your own passion.

Oh and the springtime would understand! Not a place
would fail to carry the tone of announcement.
First, the small blurted question, gradually stilled
to calmness by a day that says, clearly, "Yes!"
Then the stairs, the summoning stairs, leading up
to the fantasized temple of what's to come.
Then the quivering, the fountain, its urgent spray
already teased into falling by the promising play.

And up ahead, the summer. Not only the mornings
of summer—not only the way they change into day,
glowing before it begins. Not only the days,
so tender among the flowers and, overhead,
so intensely powerful in the shapes of the trees.
Not only the deep affection of these unharnessed forces,
not only the walks, not only the meadow at evening,
not only, after a late thunderstorm, the clarity of breath,
not only approaching sleep, and the feeling
of anticipation, the evenings . . .
                                but the nights!
The tall nights of summer, and the stars,
the stars of the earth. Oh just once to be dead
and to know them forever, all the stars: for how, then,
how—how could we forget them!

There. See. I've called the lover. But not only
*she* would come. Other girls would rise from untenable

graves and present themselves. For how could I qualify
the call, once it's gone out? The buried are always
seeking the earth again. You children—
understand one thing here and now, and it will count
for a lot. Don't believe that destiny is anything more
than what you can pack into childhood: how often
you're tempted to outdo the loved one, panting,
panting for the happy chase—after nothing, into nowhere!
Just being here is glorious. Even you knew that,
you girls who seemingly missed out on life and sank down
into the vilest streets of the city, that fester
like open sewers. For each of you had an hour—
maybe not quite an hour—some immeasurable span of time,
a distance between two whiles—in which you really existed.
Totally. Veins glutted with existence.
But we so easily neglect a thing because our neighbor
laughs at it or refuses to appreciate it or envy it.
We want something visible, something we can show,
forgetting that even the most visible joy
becomes visible only when we've transformed it, inside.

Love, the world can exist only inside, nowhere else.
Our life goes by in changing. And what's outside
invariably disappears, little by little.
Where a solid house once stood, some fantastic structure
springs up in front of it, all wrong, so completely
a product of the mind that it might as well

have stayed in the mind. The spirit of the times
builds vast warehouses of power, shapeless
as the desperate haste which it finds in all things.
It doesn't know about temples any more, those extravagant
projects of the heart. We have to preserve them
secretly now. Yes, and even when one of them manages
to survive—or anything we once prayed to, or reverenced,
or knelt before—it passes, just as it is,
into the invisible world. Many no longer see it,
and pass up the chance to rebuild it now, inside,
with pillars and statues—more magnificent than ever!

Each slow turn of the world leaves behind the disinherited,
those who own neither what's been or what's coming next.
For even what's coming next is a long way off for humans.
This shouldn't confuse us; it should make us more determined
to preserve the form we can still recognize:
this once *stood* in the human world, stood up to fate,
the annihilator, stood in the face of not knowing
where it was going, as though it existed,
and bent stars around it out of the knowing heaven.
Angel, I can still show it to you—there!

If you look it will stand rescued at last, upright
once and for all. Pillars, pylons, the Sphynx,
and—grey, striving to lift itself out of the crumbling
or foreign city—the cathedral. The miracle of it!

O look at it, Angel, for this is what we are—*us!*
You who are stronger—tell them that *this*
is what we can do: my breath is too short to praise it!

And so, after all, we haven't completely neglected to use
these spaces, these huge spaces, these spaces that are *ours*.
(How incredibly huge they must be if, after thousands
of years of our feelings, they still aren't filled.)
But even one tower was a great achievement, wasn't it?
*Great*, Angel—even compared to you. Chartres was great,
and music reached higher still, towering above us.
But even one girl in love—alone by her window
at night—just one—oh, didn't she reach
to your knee?
                    Don't think I'm courting you.
And even if I were, Angel, you wouldn't come.
For my mating call is always full of "Go back!"
Against such a strong current, you couldn't make
any headway. My call is like an outstretched arm.
And though its open hand reaches up to grasp even you,
the inapprehensible, it remains in front of you—
as defense and warning—open, wide open.

## Eighth Elegy

Animals see the open with their whole eyes.
Only our eyes, turned inward, surround it
like traps, trying to hinder its freedom of movement.
That it's out there at all we learn only
from the faces of animals. For even the eyes
of small children we turn around to our own
arrangement of things, away from the open
that shines in an animal's eyes, free from death.
Only *we* see death. The animal is free
and carries his death always behind him,
just as before him he carries God,
so that when he moves he moves into always,

as a brook moves. Never, not for a single day,
do we have before us that pure space the flowers
continually open into. For us it's always a World,
and never a Nowhere without the No—a pure,
unguarded space you can breathe and fully realize
and not be longing after. The way a child
will lose itself in the silence sometimes
and have to be shaken out of it. Or another
dies, and *is* it. For as death approaches
we no longer see it, but stare outward at last,
perhaps with the wide gaze of animals.
Lovers, although they block each other's view,
come close to it, and are amazed—they catch a glimpse
of it, almost by accident, around each other's body.
But neither steps aside, and it's a World again.

Always watching creation, we manage to see only
reflections of the free and open, made cloudy by us.
Or maybe an animal, incapable of speech, lifts its head
and quietly sees right through us. This
is what our destiny is: to stand opposite,
and nothing else, to stand opposite always.

If this animal approaching us from the opposite
direction thought the way we do, he would force
us to his way. But to him his existence is absolute,
beyond grasp, and without a sense of its own condition—

pure, like his outward gaze. And where we see the Future,
he sees the all, and himself in the all,
and is complete forever.

And yet there is in this warm alert creature
the weight and care of a great sadness.
For it clings to him too, and always, this thing
that overwhelms us: the ability to remember,
the sense that what we're striving after now
was once much nearer, more true, and knew us
in ways that were infinitely tender. Here
everything is distance, and there it was breath.
Compared to that first home, the second
is makeshift and drafty. Oh the bliss
of certain tiny creatures—the ones that always
*remain* in the womb, though the womb delivers them!
The joy of the gnat, who, hopping, remains
*within*, even when it mates. For the all *is*
its womb. And consider the half-assurance
of the bird, who, from the manner of its conception,
almost understands both. For like the soul
of a dead Etruscan it finds itself in a space,
yes, but one upon which its own image
rests as a lid. And how confusing to leave a womb
and have to fly! As though afraid of itself
it stumbles through the air, like a crack
going through a cup. Like the path of a bat

through the porcelain of evening.

And we: the watchers, always, everywhere,
looking toward the all and never from it!
It overpowers us. We arrange it. It falls apart.
We arrange it again. We ourselves fall apart.

Who has turned us around this way, so that,
no matter what we do, we look as though we're leaving?
Like someone standing for the last time
on the last hill from which he can view
his whole valley—the way he turns, stops, lingers—
this is the way we live, forever leaving.

## Ninth Elegy

Why—when we might have been laurel trees,
a little darker than all the other greens,
with tiny curves at the edge of every leaf
like the smiles of a wind—why, then,
did we have to be made human, so that
denying our destiny, we still long for it?

Certainly not because happiness really exists,
that quick gain of an approaching loss.
Not to experience wonder or to exercise the heart.
The laurel tree could have done all that.

But because just being here matters, because
the things of this world, these passing things,
seem to need us, to put themselves in our care
somehow. Us, the most passing of all.
Once for each, just once. Once and no more.
And for us too, once. Never again. And yet
it seems that this—to have once existed,
even if only once, to have been a part
of this earth—can never be taken back.

And so we keep going, trying to achieve it,
trying to hold it in our simple hands,
our already crowded eyes, our dumbfounded hearts.
Trying to become it. And yet who do we plan
to give it to? True, we'd rather keep it all
ourselves, forever. But into that other state
what can be taken across? Not the ability to see,
which we learn here so slowly, and not anything
that's happened here. None of it. And so,
the pain. And so, before everything else,
the weariness. The long business of love.
Only the completely indescribable things.

But later, under the stars—what good would it do
anyway, then, to describe these things?
For the traveler doesn't bring back
from the mountainside to the valley

a handful of earth, which would explain nothing
to anyone, but rather some acquired word, pure,
a blue and yellow gentian. And are we here,
perhaps, merely to say: *house, bridge, fountain,*
*gate, jar, fruit tree, window*—at most,
*pillar, tower*? But to *say* them, you understand—
to say them in such a way that even the things
themselves never hoped to exist so intensely.
Isn't the sly earth's secret purpose,
when it urges two lovers on, that all of creation
should share in their shudder of ecstasy?
A doorsill: the simple way two lovers
will wear down the sill of their door a little—
they too, besides those who came before
and those who will come after. . .gently.

Here is the time for what you can say,
this is its country. Speak and acknowledge.
More than ever things are falling away—
the things that we live with—and what is replacing them
is an urge without image. An urge whose crusts
will crumble as soon as it grows too large
and tries to get out. Between the hammerblows
our heart survives—just as the tongue, even
between the teeth, still manages to praise.

Praise, but tell the angel about the world,

not the indescribable. You can't impress him
with your lofty feelings; in the universe,
where he feels with far greater feeling, you're
just a beginner. So show him some simple thing,
something that's fashioned from generation to generation
until it becomes really ours, and lives near our hand,
and in our eyes. Tell him about the things.
He'll stand there amazed, the way you stood
beside the rope-maker in Rome or the potter on the Nile.
Show him how happy a thing can be, how innocent
and ours, how even the groan of sorrow decides
to become pure form, and serves as a thing
or dies in a thing, escaping to the beyond,
ecstatic, out of the violin. And these things,
that live only in passing, they understand
that you praise them. Fleeting, they look to us,
the most fleeting, for help. They hope that within
our invisible hearts we will change them entirely into—
oh endlessly—into *us*! Whoever we finally are.

Earth, isn't this what you want, to rise up in us
invisible? Isn't it your dream to be someday
invisible? Earth! Invisible! If not this change,
what do you ask for so urgently? Earth, loved one,
I will. Believe me, you don't need any more
of your springtimes to win me: one
is already more than my blood can take.

For as long as I can remember, I've been yours
completely. You've always been right,
and your most sacred idea is that death
is an intimate friend.

Look: I live. But from where do I draw this life,
since neither childhood nor the future grows less. . . ?
More being than I can hold springs up in my heart!

# Tenth Elegy

Someday, leaving the grim vision behind,
may I celebrate and praise assenting angels!
May I strike the keys with precision, and may none
of the heart's hammers fall on slack or uncertain
or breaking strings. May the tears that stream down
my face make me more radiant, and may those
that are less conspicuous bloom.

And how I will cherish you then, you nights
of grieving, sisters I couldn't console.
How I wish I had gone on my knees more freely,
surrendered myself more loosely to your loosened hair.

Sorrows—how we waste them! How we keep looking ahead
at their sad length, to see if maybe they'll end.
When really they're nothing more than our winter foliage,
our dark evergreen, just one of the seasons
of your hidden year—and not only season,
but setting, settlement, campground, the place we live.

But the real city of pain—how strange the streets
are there—the steady roar that passes for stillness,
the swaggering crumbling monument to Confusion,
cast from the mold of inanity, and painted gold.
How an angel would trample to dust their marketplace
of comforts, just alongside the ready-made
purchased church, as clean and shut and bewildered
as a post office on Sunday. And on the outskirts,
circling the town like a border, is the town fair.
Roller coasters of Freedom! High-divers and jugglers
of Enthusiasm! And the lifelike shooting galleries
where Luck is dressed to kill, and where the targets
fall over with a tinny sound when a marksman
happens to hit one. Then, leaving the cheers,
he staggers on to try his luck elsewhere;
for the booths are calling all the curious,
the barkers are barking, the drums drumming.
And then there's the real treat—for adults only:
the sex-life of money! the anatomical techniques—
and not just for amusement! The genitals of gold—

everything, the whole works, the real facts!
Educational! Guaranteed to increase fertility!

Oh but just beyond all this, behind the last billboard—
the one with the ads for "Deathless," the bitter beer
that beer-drinkers find sweet as long as they munch
on plenty of fresh distractions—just behind
that billboard, right in back of it, everything's *real*!
Children are playing and lovers are holding each other—
over there, seriously, in the sad-looking grass
where the dogs obey their nature.

The young man walks on, still drawn by something—
perhaps by the love of some young Sorrow.
He follows behind her into the meadow. She says:
it's still far; we live way out there . . .
                                    Where?
But the young man follows. He's stirred by the way
she carries herself. Her shoulders, her neck—
perhaps she comes from a line of nobility.
Still, he leaves her, he turns around, looks back,
waves. . . . What's the use? She's a sorrow.

Only those who die young follow her lovingly,
and they only in the earliest stage of eternity,
when they're being weaned from earth. She waits
for the girls and becomes their friend, gently

showing them what she wears: the pearls of grief
and the finely spun veils of patience.
With the boys she merely walks, silent.

But later, in the valley where they live,
one of the older Sorrows answers the boy's questions.
Once, she says, we were a great family, we Sorrows.
Our fathers worked the mines deep in those mountains.
Even still, among humans, you'll sometimes find
a polished fragment of primeval pain or,
from an old volcano, a petrified slag of anger.
Yes, that came from up there. Once, we were rich.

And she leads him lightly through the broad countryside
of Sorrow, shows him the temple columns or the ruins
of those castles where the lords of Sorrow once ruled
the land wisely. Shows him the tall trees of tears
and the fields where sadness blossoms, known to the living
only as tender leaves; shows him the herds of grief
as they graze. And sometimes a bird gets frightened
and breaks across their line of vision, spelling out
the long written word of its lonely cry. In the evening
she takes him out to the graves of the elders
of the House of Sorrows, the sybils and the prophets.
But as night comes on, they wander more slowly,
and after awhile that other tombstone, the moon, rises
and watches over everything, brother to the one that watches

over the Nile—the Sphynx—with a face like a secret chamber.
And they marvel at that head with its regal corona,
marvel at how, quietly and forever, it has set
a human face on the scale of the stars.

Dizzy from just having died, he can't quite focus it.
But her glance scares an owl up behind the corona's rim.
And the bird, slowly brushing the moon's cheek
at the roundest and ripest curve, faintly traces
on the new hearing powers of the dead boy,
as on the pages of an open book, the indescribable outline.

And higher, the stars. New ones. The stars
of the land of grief. She names them slowly: "There, look—
The Horseman, The Rod. And that fuller constellation
is called The Wreath of Fruit. And further over,
toward the pole: Cradle, Path, The Burning Book,
Doll, Window. And in the southern sky,
pure as if held in the palm of a sacred hand,
the clear, brilliant 'M,' which stands for Mothers. . . ."

But the dead boy must go on. Silently, the older Sorrow
brings him as far as the wide ravine where,
there in the moonlight, it shimmers: the Spring of Joy.
She names it reverently, adding: "In the human world,
it is an enduring stream."

They stand at the foot of the mountains
and she embraces him, weeping.

Alone, he climbs to the mountains of primeval pain,
and not once do his footsteps make a sound
as he follows his soundless fate.

And yet if the endlessly dead were to try to awaken us,
to tell us what it's like, they'd point perhaps
to the catkins of the leafless hazel, those small flowers
that hang down, or maybe they'd mean the rain
that falls to the black earth in early spring—

and we, because we always think of happiness as *rising*,
would feel an emotion very close to alarm,
the one we always feel when a happy thing
*falls*.

Gary Miranda was born in Bremerton, Washington, and was raised in the Pacific Northwest. His poems have appeared in many magazines, among them *The New Yorker*, *The Atlantic Monthly*, and *Poetry*. His first book of poetry, *Listeners at the Breathing Place*, won the Princeton Series of Contemporary Poets Competition and was published in 1978. He is currently Writer-In-Residence at Reed College in Portland, Oregon.

This book has been designed and printed by John Laursen at Press-22 during the autumn of 1981. The illustration is from a woodcut by Anita Bigelow. The Palatino type is by Irish Setter. 1600 copies have been produced in the first printing, of which 100 have been bound in cloth over boards with a leather spine and numbered and signed by the translator. This is number 86